COR

Ghost Stories

Prepare to be frightened by these terrible
tales from around Cornwall

BRADWELL
BOOKS

Published by Bradwell Books
9 Orgreave Close Sheffield S13 9NP
Email: books@bradwellbooks.co.uk

British Library Cataloguing in Publication Data: a catalogue
record for this book is available from the British Library.
1st Edition

ISBN: 9781902674476

Edited by Louise Maskill

Print: Gomer Press, Llandysul,
Ceredigion SA44 4JL
Design by: JenksDesign@yahoo.co.uk

CONTENTS

CORNWALL'S HAUNTED COUNTRYSIDE

INTRODUCTION

Many people were introduced to ghosts by Charles Dickens in *A Christmas Carol*, with the Ghost of Christmas Past, followed by the Ghost of Christmas Present, and finally the Ghost of Christmas Yet to Come. *A Christmas Carol* was published on 19 December 1843. Earlier in 1843 Charles Dickens had visited Cornish tin mines where he saw children working in appalling conditions, an experience that was later reflected in his writing. One might also wonder whether he heard tales of the ghosts that inhabit Cornish tin mines. These ghosts are known as Knockers, and are said to be the spirits of Jews who crucified Christ and were forced to work in Cornish tin mines as punishment.

Ghosts seem to take many forms, appearing at different times in the most unlikely of places and haunting all manner of people. First, let's establish what a ghost is. One belief is that a ghost is the soul or spirit of a deceased person or animal that can appear in a visible form or other manifestation, and this apparition can be seen or sometimes heard by the living. There are many tales of people encountering figures that are recognisable as their loved ones, who later turn out to have died at the moment of the apparition. These figures may be clear and distinct or hazy and blurred, but most trigger an emotion in the people who see them – sometimes fear or confusion, but more often love, peace, calm or a feeling of needing to be in touch with that person.

Other types of ghost seem to be bound to specific places, times or environmental conditions, such as the spirits that remain in the houses they have loved, anniversary ghosts that can be seen on particular days of the year (often the date of their death), or the phantom ships that patrol offshore during dark stormy nights. Meanwhile, some ghosts seem intent only on mischief, banging and thumping in the dead of night and sometimes even moving or throwing items.

The sea and the River Tamar almost make Cornwall an island and give it a real feeling of being Celtic, which helps to maintain its unique atmosphere of myth and magic. The Duchy of Cornwall is known internationally for its ghosts, and many consider it to be the most haunted place in Britain, with the area's rich legend and folklore creating the perfect backdrop for the creepy happenings in Celtic Kernow. In this book the haunting of famous places like St Michael's Mount, Roche Rock, Jamaica Inn and Pengersick Castle will be recounted. Eerie sounds of bells and the heavy tread of the boots of deceased miners will be described. Locations of all manner of manifestations, from headless horses to a white rabbit, will be revealed. We will also encounter stories of sightings that turn out to be somewhat less spooky than was first thought when the truth is revealed.

However, it is worth repeating what the novelist Anna Elizabeth Bray (1826–1874) was quoted as saying: *A real old Cornish house without a ghost is an impossibility, and the true believer in the mystical will scorn the prosaic idea of rats as a solution to mysterious sound...* In October 1885 the Royal Cornwall Gazette printed the following, which is also worth noting:

Advice on the subject of ghost-seeing given by a hardened sceptic to a young friend – My dear boy, if a ghost comes in at the door, take a pistol; if he comes up from the floor, take a pill.

Ghostly experiences may happen to anyone, even the most sceptical. In a large majority of cases where ghosts are clearly seen or heard, a definite sensation of cold has been experienced. If you are still waiting for your first ghostly encounter, enjoy reading about the occurrences in this book. To believe or not to believe is the question; some answers may lie in this journey to discover ghost stories old and new.

GHOSTS ALONG CORNISH COASTS

There are nearly three hundred miles of remarkable Cornish coastline, including dramatic cliffs, secret coves, spectacular beaches, breathtaking bays and amazing surf. The coastal scenery is varied and beautiful. As well as everything nature offers there are picturesque fishing villages, engine houses, castles, inns, hotels and lighthouses.

Before eerie stories from different Cornish coastal locations are related, it is worth mentioning a type of haunting that happens around the shores where there have been shipwrecks and fatalities. The souls of drowned sailors appear to haunt these places and the calling of the dead is often heard. Many a fisherman has declared he has heard the voices of dead sailors calling their own names, perhaps in an effort to remind the living of their watery fate.

BOSCASTLE

Situated on the north Cornish coast in King Arthur country, Boscastle will always be remembered for the flash flooding in 2004. It also hosts the world's largest collection of witchcraft-related artefacts and regalia in the Museum of Witchcraft, which certainly implies supernatural links. The museum was investigated for ghosts in 2011 by the Cornish Paranormal Group, but although the investigation noted a spooky atmosphere, nothing of significance was recorded.

However, there appears to be plenty of ghostly activity at the Wellington Hotel in Boscastle, a sixteenth century coaching

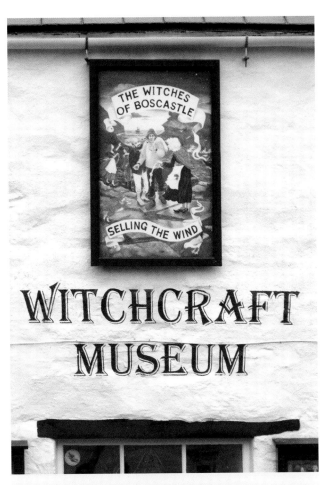

Witchcraft Museum, Boscastle

The Wellington Hotel (the Welly) Boscastle

inn known locally as the Welly. Victor Tobutt, a former owner of the Wellington Hotel, once saw a very lifelike eighteenth century coachman with his hair tied back, dressed in a fancy shirt, frock coat and boots. The coachman disappeared by walking through a solid wall. Several of the staff also confirmed that they had seen the ghost of the coachman.

There seems to be more than one ghost haunting the Wellington Hotel. The figure of a young lady jilted by a lover has been seen to jump through an upper window, apparently to her death.

As if this was not enough paranormal activity for one hotel, in the rooms numbered nine and ten there have been sightings of

The Napoleon Inn Pub Sign, Boscastle

another ghost, an old woman who sometimes sits on the beds and walks through closed doors.

Not to be out-haunted, the Napoleon Inn in Boscastle is home to a poltergeist who likes move small objects, make pictures fall and tug at people's clothing. The poltergeist has the apt nickname of Plucker.

The Napoleon Inn, Boscastle

ST MICHAEL'S MOUNT

This small island in Mount's Bay in west Cornwall can be reached by ferry when the tide is in, and by vehicle or on foot along the causeway from Marazion when the tide is out. St Michael's Mount is often referred to as the jewel in Cornwall's crown. Its Cornish name is *Karrek Loos y'n Koos*, the grey rock in the woods.

As would be expected, the romantic and mysterious St Michael's Mount, whose very name comes from an appearance by St Michael to local fisherman in AD 495, has incidents of a paranormal nature linked to it.

St Michael's Mount

The Grey Lady is a ghost that has been seen by many in the stone-built castle at the top of St Michael's Mount. She is believed to be a maid who worked there and fell in love with a resident, only to be jilted at the altar. The maid was so distraught that she ran down the Long Passage, from where she climbed out onto a wall and threw herself to her death on the rocks at the bottom of the Mount. The Grey Lady now haunts the Long Passage, running down it before disappearing out of the window at the end.

Another inexplicable occurrence is connected with one of the Mount's grandest bedrooms, containing a four-poster bedstead decorated with Spanish ships wrecked off the Cornish coasts. It is said that no child has ever managed to have a good night's sleep in this bed.

Sign at the boundary of Marazion

MARAZION

The town of Marazion, situated on the shore of Mount's Bay, is widely famed as the gateway to St Michael's Mount. The story of the ghost of an unknown lady who frequents the Marazion Green area of the town is well attested; she is known to hitch a ride on a horse and gallop as far as the nearby Red River before disappearing. This same lady has often been described as ghostly white when she has materialised to accompany late-night walkers before fading away into the darkness.

LOOE

This small coastal town in the southeast of Cornwall is a busy port and a favourite location for holidaymakers who enjoy the sandy beaches. The town is divided in two by the River Looe, creating East Looe and West Looe.

Hopefully not many visiting tourists will have seen the ill omen of a white hare in the town, running down the hill at Talland and vanishing when it reaches the Jolly Sailor, a West Looe inn known locally as the Jolly and which is one of the oldest pubs in the country. The white hare haunting is said to be related to a young lady who committed suicide.

Another apparition seen in this location is a coachman with a ponytail who wears a ruffled shirt. Finally, on a slightly different tack, it is also worth looking out to sea from the beach at Looe, because in 1949 a pair of green sea monsters resembling Chinese dragons were observed chasing fish.

ST AGNES

St Agnes is an atmospheric village on the north Cornish coast, with a rich mining history. St Agnes is featured in *Popular Romances of the West of England* by Robert Hunt (1807–1887) in connection with the legend of the Giant Bolster, who was so tall he could stand with one foot on St Agnes Beacon and the other foot on Carn Brea, a distance of six miles.

Another story is very relevant to this book on Cornish ghosts; it concerns Dorcas, the spirit of Polbreen Mine which is situated at the foot of St Agnes Beacon. Little is known about the life of Dorcas. She lived in one of the small cottages adjoining the mine, and it is thought that her husband died in a mining accident. One night shortly after her tragic loss she committed suicide by flinging herself down the deep mine shaft. Her dead and broken body was discovered the next day, brought to the surface and eventually buried. However, it seems something of her remained in the mine.

In the working days of the mine the presence of Dorcas was very apparent. She appeared to take a malicious delight in tormenting hard-working miners, calling them by name and luring away from their tasks. Apparently this was done so often that if a miner working on the tribute system (based on profit sharing from the sales of the ore raised in the mine) had a low month's wages, he was accused of chasing Dorcas.

The haunting of the deceased widow usually only took the form of a voice calling, her sad tones echoing along the long damp passageways. However, there were some miners working in Polbreen who said they had seen her. It is considered an unquestionable local fact that more than one man who met the spirit in the mine had his clothes torn off his back; whether this was done maliciously or in fun is unclear.

However, not all the things attributed to Dorcas are bad. On one occasion she acted kindly and kept calling a miner by

Wheal Coates, St Agnes

name until he left his workplace to go and see who the voice belonged to. He had not gone far when a mass of rock weighing many tons fell from the roof at the point where he had been standing. If the miner had not gone when Dorcas called, he would have surely been buried alive.

In the garden of the Railway Inn in St Agnes a shaft from Polbreen Mine can be found. A ghostly figure, assumed to be that of Dorcas, has been seen emerging from the shaft and going into the pub. Despite her loss the spectre is still mischievous, with a liking for moving pictures on the wall of the Railway Inn.

Another mine near St Agnes that is also believed to be haunted is Wheal Coates. This mine goes down to the sea, and legend states that the mine is haunted by the ghosts of the men who died working in these severe and dangerous conditions.

LAND'S END

Crashing waves and rugged cliffs are characteristic of the most westerly point in Britain. It is magnificent – truly a sight to take the breath away. Looking out across the Atlantic Ocean, on a clear day the Isles of Scilly some twenty-eight miles distant are visible on the horizon.

You might think that the geographical splendour of Land's End is not quite the setting for ghostly happenings of the kind

Land's End, from where the eerie peal of bells from Lyonesse can be heard

related in this book. However, look again out across the Atlantic towards the Isles of Scilly. Imagine the mythical lost land of Lyonesse referred to in Arthurian literature – an area of great fertility and piety that was once united with the Isles of Scilly and western Cornwall. It is said that no less than 140 churches stood in a region that is now the seabed. This land beneath the sea has inspired many poetic descriptions, among them *Sunk Lyonesse* by Walter de la Mare and *When I set out for Lyonesse* by Thomas Hardy.

Visit Land's End and take a boat trip when the sea is rough. Listen to the sound of the sea and watch out for the eerie peal of bells from churches in Lyonesse beneath the waves.

Welcome to Land's End

The next story, which concerns the haunting manifestation of a dog in the vicinity of Land's End, starts in the sixteenth century. To honour Queen Elizabeth I the Emperor of China sent a Pekingese dog and bitch to England accompanied by a royal princess. The dog was allowed to roam freely on the ship, but the bitch was kept for safety in a large and beautifully carved ivory chest. During the voyage five puppies were born. The crew of the ship believed the princess was a demon in disguise, and they thought the valuable box contained treasure rather than a dog. Crossing the sea on the last stage of the journey from France to Britain a storm blew up. The crew blamed the storm on the princess, and their interest in the ivory chest increased. Several of the ship's crew decided to go to the cabin of the princess and investigate. When one of the crew attempted to take the chest, the Pekingese dog bit him. The rest of the crew took instant revenge and cast the chest and the princess over the side of the ship into the turbulent sea. Sure enough, the storm began to subside as they approached the Cornish coastline.

Later, at Land's End, a local man found the dead princess' body together with the chest full of dead puppies. He was amazed to find that the Pekingese bitch was still alive, but she was close to death. The man dug a grave and buried the princess and the box of puppies. He placed the dying dog by the grave and went to get food and water for her. When he returned, however, the last remaining Pekinese dog had vanished.

When the ship docked, word spread about the supposed treasure of the princess. Many set out to look for it. The crewman who had been bitten died suddenly. A rumour began to spread about the power of the dog bite, and those who found the grave of the princess avoided going near it for fear of the same fate.

A young boy out beachcombing in the mid-eighteenth century stumbled upon a small piece of the ivory box. As he held it the boy felt a bite on his hand, and he later died. The bite was said to have been that of the Pekingese, now known as the Daisy Dog and forever sworn to protect the royal princess.

Today locals living near the area of the grave of the princess say that an intense cold surrounds it, and it is protected by the spirit of her dead dog. If anyone tries to disturb the princess' last resting place they will be bitten by the phantom guard dog and the bite will result in their death.

HELL'S MOUTH

The cliffs above Hell's Mouth are one of the highest points in the area, standing at around 290 feet with a sheer drop to the sea. This dramatic cliff formation between Portreath and Gwithian is a notorious suicide spot, giving rise to the belief that it is haunted. It is said that the screams of a man who committed suicide by leaping off the cliff can be heard when stormy weather approaches.

Hell's Mouth, an infamous suicide spot

TINTAGEL

This Atlantic coast village in north Cornwall, the location of Tintagel Castle, is well known for its association with the legends surrounding King Arthur and his Knights of the Round Table.

One story concerns the fateful day when King Arthur was killed. It is said that his spirit migrated into the body of the Cornish chough, with the red beak and feet of the bird representing the violent end of the King. The Cornish believe that now the chough has returned to Cornwall after a long absence, Arthur is ready once more to lead his people when needed.

Another great character from Arthurian legend is the wizard Merlin. A cave under Tintagel Castle is said to be one of the homes of Merlin; his presence can be felt there, and it is said he is reluctant to leave the cave.

A new haunting in Tintagel was reported in local and national newspapers in August 2012. A house once owned by Kate Winslet, star of *Titanic*, the high grossing film of 1997, was virtually destroyed by fire. The house was called Castle Minor, sitting below the King Arthur's Castle Hotel and benefitting from spectacular views. The film actress bought the property in 2001 but never moved in, and it was sold on to an ex-pat living in America.

When it was built in 1899 Castle Minor was a generating station for King Arthur's Castle Hotel, one of the first properties in the village to have electric lighting. At that time it was the home of the engineer who attended to the generators. It was believed that the engineer lived a lonely life, and when he died his ghost remained in the property. At various times people sleeping rough have been known to have bedded down in the building, but on the night of the fire it was raining and no one was seen at Castle Minor.

John Mapplin, who owns the nearby King Arthur's Castle Hotel, said it was a mystery how the fire started, but some local people believe that the fire was started by the resident ghost. When Kate Winslet bought the property the phantom engineer fell madly in love with her, and when the star sold the house the ghost could not get over the fact that it was

Castle Minor. Did the resident ghost fall in love with Kate Winslet?

unlikely she would ever return and therefore he would never see her again. Perhaps the ghost felt snubbed, and this led to the fire that destroyed the building.

POLPERRO

Polperro is a village and fishing harbour on the southeast coast, once a thriving centre for smuggling. Today it is a tourist delight with its jumble of charming cottages.

In the maze of caves at Polperro is a chamber known as Willy Willcock's Hole. This is where a fisherman of the same name got lost in the tunnels and died of starvation. His spirit is still trying to find its way out. Many claim to have seen the ghost of the lost fisherman; others who have heard the terrible screams of Willy Willcock have said the sound is terrifying. Meanwhile the Crumplehorn Inn in Polperro is supposed to be haunted by a gentler couple, thought to be a young soldier and the girl who was his lover.

SENNEN COVE

This is a coastal village where the work and bravery of the members of the Royal National Lifeboat Institution's station are greatly respected. Many who visit the area enjoy the walk from Sennen Cove to Land's End. In doing so they pass a rock known as the Irish Lady, which has a terrible story attached to it.

Long ago, an Irish ship was wrecked on the coast nearby. A lady was the sole survivor, managing to swim to a rock and haul herself to safety. Local residents knew she was clinging to the rock, but the sea was so rough and the weather so appalling that no one was able to get to her. For several days and nights local residents watched helplessly; the Irish lady clinging to the rock continued to implore someone to act, but the terrible conditions continued so that no one was able to help. Eventually she died from hunger, thirst and exposure to the elements, and her body was seen to slip into the sea. These days whenever there is a dreadful storm the ghost of the Irish lady is seen reliving her ordeal on the rock that was named after her.

The Irish Lady viewed from the cliffs at Sennen Cove

FALMOUTH

Falmouth is a town famous for its harbour. Together with Carrick Roads, it ranks as the third deepest natural harbour in the world. King Henry VIII had Pendennis Castle built in Falmouth to defend Carrick Roads. Pendennis, like many other castles, is reputed to be haunted.

Pendennis Castle, built in the reign of King Henry VIII

Cold spots have been reported in the castle armoury even on bright summer days. Be careful climbing up the staircase, for it is believed to be haunted. Sometimes screams can be heard, and a kitchen maid apparently fell to her death when carrying a tray of food up these very stairs. Another ghost is understood to wander around the Tudor kitchen.

In 1849 local newspapers reported that the people of Falmouth had been thrown into the greatest consternation by sundry strange nocturnal sounds heard and very weird sights seen. The sounds were described in many different ways – as resembling heavenly music; doleful; like someone going under painful surgery; or like the last pangs of a dreadful death. The sounds were heard all over the locality, and even more so at sea; pilots and fisherman heard them while crossing the bay from the Manacles (a treacherous group of rocks off the Lizard Peninsula) to the point at Pendennis Castle. Other seamen confirmed hearing inexplicable sounds when they were in the harbour.

Meanwhile on terra firma there were some who saw the ghostly image responsible for the sounds. Again there were many different descriptions; it looked like a cow, a dog or a cat, but many characterised it as nondescript. The colour seemed to vary from person to person: white, black, tawny, red, brown or black. The eccentric movements of the thing, coupled with everything else, led to one conclusion – it must be a ghost!

Alarm spread through the town. Was this a prelude to a dire disaster about to befall Falmouth? Children, servants and many others were scared to go to bed without a candle to sleep by. Fishermen were afraid to set out to sea for their nocturnal work. Extra police patrolled during the night. The authorities had to do something.

Everyone who had a gun agreed to go out during the hours that ghosts take their rambles on earth. There were sightings, and shots were fired at the ghost from close range, but to no avail. Someone thought it might be the dark colour of the balls of shot that made them harmless to the ghost. With nothing to lose, all the balls of shot to be used in the guns were whitened with chalk before they were loaded.

What followed proved there was wisdom in the suggestion. At around one o'clock in the morning a ghostly figure was seen. Several shots coated with the white chalk were fired, and a terrible squeal was heard. However, no one in the hunting party was prepared to inspect the corpse, if there was one, during the night.

At sunrise the hunting party ventured to the spot of the shooting, and to their surprise they found the 'ghost' to be a large fat pig belonging to the nearby Royal Hotel. There does not appear to be any record to show whether the sounds and sights ceased – perhaps the ghost was frightened off? However, if it was the pig all along, with the sounds being heard so many miles out to sea, does this give credence to the notion that pigs can fly?

ST IVES

This coastal town takes its name from the Irish Saint Ia, who floated across from Ireland on a leaf. Today St Ives is a major tourist resort with a maze of narrow cobbled streets to wander

The Island, St Ives. Is the Lady with the Lantern still here?

through. It is a major centre for art and artists, and also a town with a ghostly tale or two to tell.

The Death Ship is a phantom ship that signifies disaster. From time to time in St Ives Bay a ghostly image of a sailing ship can be seen, always appearing before a tragedy at sea.

No one knows if the Death Ship appeared as a warning before this next tale of a shipwreck off St Ives. As the ship was going under a female passenger clasped her baby in her arms, determined to get to the safety of a lifeboat manned by local fisherman who were doing everything they could to help the poor unfortunates on board the stricken vessel. The lady, with her child in her arms, jumped from the sinking ship into the stormy sea. The waves were so fierce that the child was swept from the mother's arms, never to be seen again. The mother's screams were heard above the roar of the sea.

The lady was unconscious when she was dragged aboard the lifeboat and taken to the protection of the shore. When she recovered and learned of the loss of her beloved child, she collapsed with grief and died shortly after.

During her funeral, an ethereal form of the deceased rose from the coffin and was seen to float towards the Island, a headland in St Ives. From that time she has become known as the Lady with the Lantern. Every time there is a dark stormy night, she can be seen searching for her lost child by the light of her lamp. The moving light acts as a warning to ships and many a sailor has been saved because of her ghostly activities.

PENZANCE

Situated in the shelter of Mount's Bay, the town of Penzance faces southeast onto the English Channel. The name Penzance is derived from the Cornish language name *Pen Sans* meaning holy headland, named for the chapel that once stood on the point west of the harbour. There are many very attractive buildings in the town, making it special to those with an observant eye.

A former public house that had long been uninhabited, sited near the quay in Penzance, was reputed to be haunted. In 1813 when workmen were taking the house down they discovered a human skeleton underneath the floorboards, which had clearly been there for a considerable time.

According to news reports, some of the older inhabitants of Penzance remembered a sailor who was known to be quite wealthy and who had lodged in the public house, but who had suddenly disappeared without a trace. There appeared to be little doubt that the unfortunate man had been murdered and hidden under the floorboards. Those who had experienced the feeling of the house being haunted speculated that the spirit of the dead man was trying to draw attention to the fact that he had been murdered and buried there.

The apparition of Maisie Baines, wearing a cloak and bonnet that shades her face, is seen on occasion in Chapel Street before she fades into a wall. Mrs Baines was the owner of a property in the town who hired a man to keep her home and orchard secure when she went away. When she returned unexpectedly one night, the guard thought she was an intruder and shot her.

A rather more sinister apparition is the black dog that sometimes appears in the harbour area. Apparently the dog only makes itself known to those about to die. Let's hope you don't see it…

Chapel Street, Penzance

What spirits are at the Dolphin Inn, Penzance?

A spirit in a pub is not that unusual, is it? Well, maybe it is, if the spirit in question is the ghost of an old seaman who reputedly calls at the Dolphin Inn in Penzance to make a protest against his execution by hanging for a petty crime.

In Morrab Road there used to be a surgery that was used by several doctors up until the 1960s, when it became an old people's home until 1975. During that time an indistinct figure was seen by many of the staff and residents. This figure was alleged to be the ghost of a former doctor, who still did his rounds by checking on residents in the home. No one appeared to be frightened by his presence; in fact, some said that the staff looking after the residents took greater care knowing that the phantom doctor would be checking on them.

NEWQUAY

This tourist spot is a favourite location for surfers. However, not many of the area's many summer visitors will be aware of the hauntings that have occurred in the town over the centuries.

At Trethellan Hill, ghostly sightings have been reported for many years. During an excavation for the laying of pipes to the Pentire estate in 1900 the workmen unearthed some skeletons; those that believed in the ghosts found in the discovery a confirmation of their belief.

In the area around Barrowfields a headless horseman has been noted. Horse and rider appear to travel above the ground. Meanwhile, Trerice Manor, on the outskirts of Newquay at Kestle Mill, is an Elizabethan manor house with a delightful garden. A guide book from the very early twentieth century describes Trerice as *an ancient baronial mansion, which the country people still declare to be haunted by the spirit of the certain passionate Lord of Arundell, known in the neighbouring village as the 'wicked lord'.* Fleeting glimpses of a phantom lady and the occasional whiff of perfume all add to the ambiance of the Manor House.

BEDRUTHAN STEPS

This is the name of a wonderfully rugged area a few miles east of Newquay, on the north Cornish coast. Steep steps cut into the cliff lead to a beautiful beach. Bedruthan, a giant, is

Ghostly sightings at Trethellan Hill, Newquay

Listen for ghostly sounds at Bedruthan Steps.

thought to be responsible for the rock stacks that stretch across the beach; it is said he used them as stepping-stones.

This is an area known for the ghostly sounds emanating from the site of an old iron mine. Many have said they have heard the tramp of miners' boots stanking their way to work, and down in the mine one can hear the click of the miners' picks as they chip away at the rock.

PORTREATH

The small resort of Portreath, with its sandy beach and narrow harbour, was once a coastal port from which tin was shipped to South Wales. The ships then returned with coal to fire the steam engines used in the Cornish mines.

Portreath has many links to the sea, and this includes the ghosts that are purported to frequent this idyllic village. A small stone-built shelter at the top of some steps at the harbour entrance was once a pilot's lookout, but at times it also doubled as a mortuary for bodies recovered from the sea. It is known locally as the Dead Man's Hut. Shadowy figures observed in the area at night are thought to be the apparitions of unknown drowned sailors, buried in unnamed graves and unable to fully pass over; perhaps some of these poor souls come back in the hope that a family member will be able to identify them.

One cottage near the beach in Portreath is a scene of mystery and intrigue. Built in the 1600s, it is said to have been the home of smugglers who plied their trade in days of old. In the 1950s the dwelling was being altered, and the work exposed a secret room complete with an old chest, a rusty sword, a table, and a chair with a skeleton sitting in it who was wearing the remains of what appeared to be a tattered black cloak around his shoulders.

Today local residents speak of a small man in his twenties, dressed in eighteenth century clothing, who emerges in the

Dead Man's Hut, Portreath

first floor corridor out of the wood panelling which conceals a tunnel to the beach (now blocked off for security).

The unknown figure proceeds in a furtive manner towards the staircase and then vanishes.

PRAA SANDS

Praa Sands is a coastal village between Helston and Penzance in west Cornwall, well worth a visit if only for its mile-long sandy beach, which has good waves and is therefore very popular with surfers.

Allegedly one of the most haunted buildings in Cornwall is the nearby Pengersick Castle, which has stood on this site since the Middle Ages. The original twelfth century building was modified to become a fortified Tudor manor around 1500. With its well-publicised spooky reputation Pengersick Castle is a magnet drawing ghost hunters and those interested in the paranormal from around the world.

A dark story from the rich Pengersick tapestry is the reported lifestyle of one of the owners, Henry Pengersick, who died in 1343. Henry is reputed to have killed a monk, and visits from a monk-like figure presumed to be his victim are often seen in and around the Castle and grounds. It is also claimed that Henry Pengersick wounded a local vicar.

Another owner by the name of Millington, who owned the property during the reign of Henry VIII, tried to poison his wife. The story goes that she was aware he had put poison into her drink, so when he wasn't looking she changed the drinks around and Mr Millington ended up poisoning himself. The shock of this disaster seems to keep Mr Millington within the confines of Pengersick; it appears his miserable ghost wanders the castle still.

With a turbulent past like this, I wonder whether Pengersick's reputation has also drawn other ghosts into the spotlight, or whether they are just a creation of the active imaginations of visitors to the area. There are many other examples of paranormal activity that are alleged to be connected with Pengersick:

A demon dog with shining red eyes is seen near a bedroom fireplace.

A lady dressed in white is often seen in one of the bedrooms. Two women haunt another room; one is seen standing by the window, the other one is on the bed.

Several ghosts of sailors who could have survived shipwrecks have been seen abroad in the grounds of Pengersick. If a ship was sunk by the action of wreckers, any survivors were killed to conceal the evidence.

Many people were buried in unconsecrated ground; their forlorn cries can be heard around the Castle at night.

The ghost of a young girl dances on the battlements, and has been known to try to push people off if she disapproves of them.

Inexplicable sounds of footsteps have been heard.

Orbs (floating lights) have been seen on numerous occasions.

Whatever the truth of these tales, Pengersick Castle remains an atmospheric and beautiful place that is well worth a visit.

PADSTOW

Padstow is a town and fishing port on the north Cornwall coast. Famous for its Obby Oss festival, Padstow appears to be more popular than ever with visitors, perhaps due to the numerous fish-related businesses of Rick Stein, the celebrity chef. The town is situated on the west bank of the River Camel, and is well worth visiting.

The grand Prideaux Place, finished in 1592, has been the home of the Prideaux-Brune family for over four hundred

The grand Prideaux Place, Padstow

years. This classical building appears to also be the home of a small child who has been spotted running into the pantry but never comes out again. Another Prideaux ghost is the spirit of Honor Fortescue, wife of Humphrey Prideaux, who threw herself off the upper balcony following the death of her husband. Her tragic apparition is said to chase people out of bedrooms in the house.

On 18 October 1900 the Royal Cornwall Gazette reported a ghost story circulating around Padstow. Skeletons unearthed at the ancient cemetery at Harlyn Bay were displayed at a fête in the grounds of Prideaux Place. The story claimed that one of these skeletons had clothed itself, or had somehow been clothed, in a white sheet and had been seen walking near the White Gate. However, the story did not catch on, probably owing to the brilliant light cast by the gas lamp later fixed near the spot by the council. Ghosts, in popular opinion, seem to regard darkness and a white sheet as essential to their existence.

The White Hart in the town also has a haunting presence who goes by the name of Wilfred. It is suggested that he was a former priest who died there many years ago. In the White Hart the sounds of footsteps walking down the stairs and a rasping sound that comes from one of the bedrooms are considered to be further evidence of this ghostly manifestation.

PORTHTOWAN

The Cornish name for this small village is *Porth Tewyn*, meaning a cove of sand dunes, and this is an apt description. This area on the north Cornwall coast is another favourite with surfers; at low tide the beach stretches for well over a mile.

A ghostly ship has been seen anchored offshore. A voice can be heard to whisper: *The hour has come but not the man.* Suddenly, a shadowy figure races down a nearby hill and into the sea and starts heading towards the phantom ship. Whether this ghostly ship has any links to the *Rose of Devon* that sank off Porthtowan in November 1897 is unknown.

CORNWALL'S HAUNTED COUNTRYSIDE

So far our journey around the Cornish coastline will have revealed many signposts pointing to places inland. Some of these places may be familiar, while others may be obscure, but it is guaranteed that within a few miles of every inland village or town there will be an inexplicable tale.

In an attempt to analyse different types of haunting, this next story falls into the category of the anniversary ghost – one that seems to appear on an exact date to mark a previous event. Without naming a precise location for reasons that will become clear, this first story starts in Falmouth and ends with a shiver down the spine.

THE GIRL IN THE RAIN

During the 1950s tourist advertisements led everyone to believe that *Falmouth in Cornwall is the resort with the palm tree climate*. However, on 18 July 1952 this slogan couldn't have been more wrong. The weather was atrocious.

During a visit to his uncle, Terry Bray became so engrossed in conversation that he missed the last bus from Falmouth. Needing to get home, the eighteen-year-old borrowed a Mackintosh from his uncle, cursed the torrential downpour and started to walk.

Terry lived in a cottage midway between Falmouth and Helston. He made good time with the help of a lift as far as

Penryn. By then it was nearly eleven o'clock at night; Terry pressed on, although he was soaked by this time.

When he had walked through Longdowns, Terry noticed a young female walking ahead of him. He quickened his pace. When he could see her properly he realised she was only wearing a summer dress. Terry shouted to her. The girl paused, turned around, and waited for him to reach to her. Terry was pleasantly surprised. She was good-looking, and was probably about sixteen years of age. Without hesitation, Terry took off his uncle's Mackintosh and put it around the girl's shoulders.

Even though she was soaking wet and shivering, she gave him a lovely smile and said, 'Thank'ee, yer a gentleman.'
He was a little surprised with her very old-sounding dialect, but on the other hand he knew that in some remote spots in this area of Cornwall, Cornish dialect was still very much in evidence.

The young girl – Susie was her name – said she lived down a lane near the kiddley. Terry knew this was the old word for a pub and the next one was about a mile further on. They walked on together, the heavy rain making further conversation difficult.

When they reached the lane Susie gave Terry a quick kiss on the lips, which made him gasp. It was like being kissed by an iceberg. He thought the girl must be freezing, so he said, 'Keep the Mackintosh. I'll pick it up tomorrow.'

Susie agreed straight away, with another smile. The smile made the young man feel like a king, although he looked like a drowned rat. He asked if he could walk her to her door.

Susie hesitated, then declined, saying, 'I doan't be like that, if yew knaw what I mean.'

Terry nodded and smiled in understanding.

Susie gave him another quick kiss before she hurried off down the lane. Terry watched her until she was out of sight before he continued on his way again. He got home around midnight, changed out of his wet clothes, had a hot cup of tea, poked up the coal fire, and fell asleep in the armchair.

Terry got through his next day's work on the farm, although he was feeling really tired after the previous night. When work was over he came home and had a plate of some mouth-watering stew his mother had cooked for him, followed by apple tart. After his meal the young man's thoughts turned to Susie, and he made up his mind to go and see her.

With a spring in his step, Terry reached the lane where they had parted and started to walk down it. Eventually he came to a very old thatched cottage that looked somewhat run down and out of place in the 1950s. Nevertheless he knocked upon the door.

Old thatched cottage (used with permission of Helston Museum)

'Cum en plaise,' said a spooky voice.

Terry opened the door. Although it was a bright, sunny evening outside, he had a hard job to see into the room. He made out an old woman, sitting on a rocking chair in front of a fireplace that looked as if it had not been lit for years.

'I'm Terry Bray,' he said.

'I does knaw who yew are,' the old woman said, and cackled. 'Soosie sid yew wud be callun.'

'Is Susie here?' Terry asked.

The woman rocked back and forth in the chair and grinned. 'Me name es Molly Trembath. Soosie es me daughter, but sha's not 'ere. Sha left a message for yew ta go ta the churchyard ta see 'er. Knaw what I mean, do ee?' Molly Trembath started laughing, and kept repeating, 'Knaw what I mean, do ee?'

Terry bid Molly Trembath goodbye and hurried back up the lane. Thrilled with the thought of seeing Susie again, he soon reached the cemetery.

He couldn't see Susie anywhere. He shouted her name, but there was no response. Thinking Susie may be hiding from him, Terry started to walk round the graves looking for her. Then he noticed his uncle's Mackintosh draped over a headstone. Terry picked up the coat and saw what was written on the monument:

R.I.P.
Susie Trembath
Aged sixteen
Murdered in this Parrish
on the 18th day of July 1852

A hundred years ago yesterday, Terry thought, and felt a shiver run down his spine.

Mackintosh left on headstone of Susie Trembath

ALTARNUN

Situated on the northeastern edge of Bodmin Moor, this picturesque village is dominated by the 109-foot-tall tower of the fifteenth century church dedicated to St Nonna and known as the *Cathedral of the Moors*. Within the church there are seventy-nine remarkable wooden bench ends, carved by local craftsman Robert Daye between 1510 and 1530. Very near to the village there is a nine-stone circle that has a great atmosphere even in misty weather; it is very popular on solstice days.

Spirits of the female form have been reported in Altarnun. One, a former landlady known as Peggy, returns to the King's

Bridge over the River Altarnun

The King's Head pub sign, near Five Lanes

Head pub near Five Lanes every so often, just to check it is running smoothly and to her satisfaction.

Mary, another ghostly lady, ended her relationship with the Reverend Tripp by drowning herself in the local river. Her grey figure has been seen by the door of the old vicarage and in one of the bedrooms. Footsteps that are also heard here are thought to belong to the late Reverend.

BODMIN MOOR

Northeast of the town of Bodmin lies Bodmin Moor, a wild, dramatic and unspoiled granite landscape. The moor covers an area of eighty square miles and has been officially designated an Area of Outstanding Natural Beauty. Where possible, certain areas of the moor are used for pasture by local farmers. However, it is the natural highlights of the moor that fascinate, particularly the imposing summits of Brown Willy, standing at 1375 feet, and Rough Tor (pronounced Row Tor) at 1325 feet, the highest and second highest points in Cornwall respectively. Many watercourses flow across this landscape including the Rivers Fowey and Camel. Antiquities like the standing stones known as the Hurlers and the Pipers, along with Trethevy Quoit and the Cheesewring, all contribute to the unique atmosphere with an emphasis on myth and legend. Dozmary Pool on the moor is said to be where Sir Bedivere threw Excalibur to the Lady of the Lake in Arthurian lore, and in more recent times tales of the Beast of Bodmin Moor have been often in the news.

The sombre Dozmary Pool

In an area like this there are many stories of hauntings, and some relate to actual documented events, such as the brutal murder of an eighteen-year-old girl on the slopes of Rough Tor on 14 April 1844.

Charlotte Dymond lived in as a servant for a sixty-one-year-old widow, Phillipa Peter, at Penhale Farm, Davidstow, on the edge of the moor. Other staff for Mrs Peter included the twenty-year-old John Stevens, a personal servant, and also the slightly lame farm hand Matthew Weeks, who was twenty-two and in a relationship with Charlotte Dymond.

On the fateful day of Sunday 14 April 1844, Miss Dymond, wearing a brown bonnet, a multi-coloured dress and a red cloth shawl, left Penhale at about four o'clock in the company of Mr Weeks. However, he returned to Penhale alone at half past nine in the evening, ate a hearty supper and went to bed.

Matthew Weeks continued his work duties as usual during the following week. Charlotte Dymond still hadn't returned. The farm hand was questioned, but said he knew nothing of the whereabouts of his girlfriend. However, as soon as Weeks knew a search was being organised for the missing girl he promptly absconded.

On the Sunday following Charlotte's disappearance, John Stevens and Mrs Peter's son John found tracks which they assumed were made by the couple, but then they lost the trail. On Monday the search was renewed with a group of twelve individuals now searching for the missing servant. Footprints made by a girl and a man were found; the search continued, and they eventually found the body of the girl on a small bank by the stream of Rough Tor Ford. Charlotte Dymond lay face upwards, about a foot from where the water flowed; she looked as if she had been washed there by the water. Her throat had been savagely cut. The wound was about eight inches in length and over two inches in depth.

Charlotte Dymond's body was found on the banks of Rough Tor Ford

Charles Causley (1917–2003), the renowned Cornish poet who wrote *The Ballad of Charlotte Dymond*, described the scene:

> Her cheeks were made of honey,
> Her throat was made of flame
> Where all around the razor
> Had written its red name.

Matthew Weeks was arrested in Plymouth. Charlotte was laid to rest on 25 April 1844, and Weeks' trial commenced on 2 August the same year. The jury quickly returned a verdict of wilful murder. He was sentenced to a public hanging at Bodmin Gaol, and it was reported that over twenty thousand people came to witness the execution and the last moments of Matthew Week's time on Earth on 20 August 1844.

A granite memorial to Charlotte Dymond has been erected at the foot of Rough Tor where her body was discovered. The murder was so atrocious and so unexpected that there is little wonder that the ghost of Charlotte Dymond still haunts the place where she died.

At Bolventor is situated probably one of the world's most famous inns; this is, of course, Jamaica Inn. This was the title of Daphne du Maurier's (1907–1989) novel of wreckers and murder, first published in 1936. Alfred Hitchcock (1899–1980) also made *Jamaica Inn* into a film.

In memory of Charlotte Dymond

The ghost of a murdered sailor that is reported to turn up at Jamaica Inn is not linked to the book. He returns in the hope of finishing his pint, and at other times he has been seen sitting on a wall outside the pub – perhaps letting the effect of those finished pints wear off before he goes back to his ghostly abode. Others have noted a sense that something is not quite right in the area surrounding the inn – a feeling that one is not alone, especially in the dead hours of the night.

Another popular spot on Bodmin Moor is St Nectan's Glen, an area of beautiful woodland that is well known for its regular supernatural sightings of hooded monks. The Manor House inn, situated in the moorland village of Rilla Mill, is a place where the sound of mysterious footsteps has been heard, always seeming to come from an empty bedroom.

The largest round barrow on Bodmin Moor is Rillaton Barrow near the village of Minions. When this Bronze Age burial mound was excavated in 1837 human remains were discovered, along with grave goods including the Rillaton Gold Cup (now in the British Museum). A ghostly druid now walks the area, and whenever he meets anyone he offers them a drink from a golden cup that never seems to empty.

Cornish mines are always good for weird manifestations; it wouldn't seem right to leave Bodmin Moor without mentioning Goonzion Down mine. Here one particular shaft is named the *roaring shaft*, because of the strange sounds and bangs that apparently emanate from an empty tunnel.

BODMIN

Situated in the centre of Cornwall, Bodmin was formerly the county town until the crown court moved to Truro. St Petroc founded a monastery in the town in the sixth century. Thomas Flamank, one of the leaders of the Cornish Rebellion of 1497, was a lawyer from Bodmin, who along with Michael an Gof from St Keverne marched to Blackheath, only to be defeated by the King's army.

Bodmin Gaol was built of local granite in 1769 by French prisoners of war. It was a notorious prison that staged its share of hangings during the period from 1785 to 1909 – including the execution of Matthew Weeks, as described above. The hangings were public affairs until 1862. After this they took place behind the closed doors of the prison.

Matthew Weeks' ghost still wanders around the old gaol; his presence is sensed, and many people have reported sightings of him. A number of local residents, as well as others who have studied the details of the 1844 murder of Charlotte Dymond, believe that Weeks was innocent, and his spirit won't rest until this is publicly acknowledged.

At the magnificent Victorian edifice of Lanhydrock House, near Bodmin, taken over by the National Trust in 1953, ghosts appear to have been in residence for many years. A little old lady dressed in grey is often seen in the Long Gallery and in the Drawing Room; many who have sighted her thought she

Bodmin Gaol, built by French Prisoners of War in 1769

was a modern-day servant until they approached her and she vanished into thin air. Other ghosts have been reported in this grandiose residence, and who can blame them for wanting to enjoy such a lavish home? The opulent lifestyle of one of the unseen guests creates the aroma of cigar smoke, a phenomenon that cannot be explained.

CALSTOCK

Calstock is a large village in southeast Cornwall on the banks of the River Tamar which divides Cornwall and Devon. The impressive viaduct that carries the railway branch line from

Plymouth to Gunnislake dominates the village. A short way downriver is the Tudor manor house of Cotehele, now in the care of the National Trust. Cotehele, like many of the excellent manor houses in Cornwall, has its own reports of hauntings. An ethereal young lady dressed entirely in white is said to linger here, and phantom music has been reported in the oldest part of the manor house.

Mining was an important industry in the Calstock area, especially in the late nineteenth century after the discovery of copper in the local vicinity. Like many dangerous bygone industries, something lingers from it in the present. On one of the roads leading into Calstock a pare (group) of miners carrying candles and dressed in old-fashioned traditional work clothes has been sighted, according to local reports.

CHYSAUSTER

Two and half miles northwest of the village of Gulval, this Iron Age settlement was originally occupied around two thousand years ago. Wandering the narrow streets among the surviving stone dwellings creates a wonderful awareness of place, while the terraced gardens hint at a sense of survival. The original villagers are understood to be Cornish, and it is thought they lived at Chysauster between 100 BC and 300 AD.

From ancient times many references have been made to the build of the Cornish, who are characterised as small statured,

Advertising picture for Chysauster

short-legged and squat people. This is typified by the original villagers who are thought to haunt Chysauster, since they are said to be small men.

GODOLPHIN CROSS

This village, in the former district of Kerrier, is situated between the towns of Hayle and Helston. The main attraction at Godolphin Cross is Godolphin House and Gardens. The house is fifteenth century and was the home of the Godolphin family until the middle of the eighteenth century. The house came into the ownership of the National Trust in 2000.

The Trust has been improving access to the site. Let's hope this and other renovation work does not frighten off a phantom funeral procession that has been seen walking past the house. Another story linked to Godolphin House is a White Lady, assumed to be Margaret who was once married to the First Earl of Godolphin. She is supposed to climb out of a closet and stroll along the path towards the Chapel. It is known that Margaret died in childbirth, and it may be assumed that the phantom funeral procession is also connected with her.

An apparition of a very different nature is said to haunt Jews Lane, situated near Godolphin House. The spectre has been seen of a Jewish man who hanged himself from a nearby tree and was buried under the road. Apparently this ghost is a shape shifter, sometimes taking the form of a bull or a fiery chariot.

ST DAY

This village, situated just outside Redruth, was a former mining area and at one time it was the centre of the copper mining industry, thereby accruing considerable wealth. In the Royal Cornwall Gazette of October 1868 an interesting court case was reported.

It was based on a claim for a quarter's rent, payable on a house in St Day. The defendant stated that she and her husband were unable to live in the house because of the noise from ghosts heard every night at eleven o'clock. His Honour remarked that if he were to accept that explanation as a reason why the rent should not be paid, other unprincipled persons summoned for arrears would assign a similar reason for nonpayment of rent. He continued that better things ought to be expected of people who could read and write than to suppose that just because some rats made a noise, a house was haunted.

Can we accept the judge's verdict, or was it a ghost that plagued the tenants? If we believe what the judge said, does this also indicate that the family couldn't pay the rent and couldn't afford to poison or kill the rats by other means? Ghosts have been reported to have regular habits. Do rats also run to time?

SOUTH PETHERWIN

This village is located in eastern Cornwall about three miles from Launceston (Lanson) on the road to Liskeard. Many writers, including Daniel Defoe (1659–1731), R.S. Hawker, the Vicar of Morwenstow (1803–1875) and Robert Hunt (1807–1887), have referred to the 1665 story of *An Account of an Apparition*, recounted by the Reverend Dr John Ruddle and attested by his son the Reverend William Ruddle, who later became the Vicar of South Petherwin in 1695.

Daniel Defoe first published *An Account of an Apparition* as a pamphlet in the second edition of his *History of the Life and Adventures of Mr Duncan Campbell* in August 1720. A detailed account of the haunting was published in *The Cornish Magazine* of 1898, written by Alfred F. Robbins under the title *A Cornish Ghost Story*. This is a well-researched and logical article, especially regarding the locations of the events. Under Horse Road and Botathen House were photographed, as was the vicarage at South Petherwin.

The events concerning the apparition, as recorded by Reverend John Ruddle, begin after a funeral on Tuesday 20 June 1665. The Parson met a Mr Bligh, from Botathen, who requested that Reverend Ruddle should visit him at his home. On the following Monday Reverend Ruddle visited as promised and found another local minister also in attendance. After dinner the minister suggested a walk in the garden. During this walk the minister talked to Reverend Ruddle about the family in general, and then started to discuss the youngest son and how sad he had become. The minister continued that the poor boy believed he was haunted, and was insistent that he met with an evil spirit on the way to school, in a field about a mile from where they were talking. Reverend Ruddle and the minister were joined at this stage by the boy's parents, who confirmed everything said in the conversation that had just taken place.

The parents urged Reverend Ruddle to talk to their son; they wondered if the boy was lazy and didn't want to go to school, or perhaps he might be in love with some girl and didn't want to talk about it, or they even thought that perhaps he wanted to be in London with his brother. The Reverend agreed to see the son and discuss things with him.

During the talk that followed, the youth revealed what had been troubling him. All he wanted was for his parents to believe him and to help him. He admitted openly that he regularly saw the ghost of a woman in a field known at that time as Higher Brown Quartils (Higher Broomfield) at South Petherwin. She was named as Dorothy Dingley, a woman who had lived nearby but who had been dead for about eight years. Mr Bligh's son said that she never spoke, always left the footpath to him, and in the time it took him to cross the field she would meet him two or three times. It had been about a year since the boy had become convinced the woman was a ghost. He had changed his route to school, going via Under Horse Road, but the haunting continued and became more frightening because the ghost now met him in the narrows of the lane. Becoming terrified of the daily occurrence the boy prayed continuously to God and repeated the Scriptures aloud.

Reverend Ruddle was very impressed with the lad's ingenuity and knew he had to help him. The next day they met at five o'clock in the morning and proceeded to Higher Broomfield, which appeared to be around twenty acres in size and distant from any dwellings. When they had walked about a third of the way across the field the spectre in the shape of a woman met them and passed them by. They walked to the end of the field and then returned, but the ghost only appeared once to them. When they returned to the house Mrs Bligh was very curious. The Reverend wouldn't commit himself on how to deal with the problem, but he requested that she should not to talk to anyone about the incident.

On Monday 27 July 1665 the Parson returned to the field on his own. The ghostly shape did appear again, but she moved swiftly away before Reverend Ruddle had a chance to challenge her. During the next investigation the Blighs, their son and Reverend Ruddle met at the field and started to walk across it in a leisurely manner; they had reached halfway when the ghost appeared. It came over a stile in front of them, moving so quickly that before they could get near it the phantom figure had passed them by. The Reverend and the young lad ran after it, but the figure disappeared almost immediately out of sight.

On this occasion Reverend Ruddle had noticed two things. First, a spaniel dog that had come with them had barked and run away as the ghost went by. Second, the ghost did not walk but seem to glide over the ground. The Blighs were strangely frightened; they had known Dorothy Dingley in her lifetime and attended her funeral, and now they recognised her features in the present apparition.

Reverend Ruddle resolved to proceed on his own and 'to use such lawful means as God hath discovered, and learned men have successfully practiced in these irregular cases'.

The next morning the Reverend went out early on his own after a period of prayer and meditation in the field next to the Quartils. He stepped over the stile into the disturbed field, and he had only walked a few yards when the ghost appeared at another stile. He spoke to it in a loud voice in the prescribed way of dealing with such occurrences. The ghost drew near to him and he spoke to the apparition again, whereupon she answered in a voice that was not audible or intelligible. Reverend Ruddle was not afraid; he spoke again, and persisted until he got an answer from the ghost that gave him satisfaction.

However, the work that had to be done was not finished on this occasion. The Reverend and the apparition met again in the same spot that evening. After a few words on each side the apparition quietly vanished and was never seen or ever troubled anyone again.

It has been suggested that the story of the haunting and the exorcism may have been written by Daniel Defoe. However, in the Cornish Magazine of 1898, Alfred F. Robbins states that the story was from the original manuscript of John Ruddle. Mr Robbins backed this up by stating that there is a manuscript copy of the story signed by John Ruddle, and after the signature it reads: *This is a copy of w^t I found written by my father John Ruddle. Taken by me William Ruddle.* The final comment about this remarkable story may be summed up in a quote from Alfred F. Robbins: *The completeness of the body of proof of the Ruddle authorship leaves nothing therefore to be desired.*

David Trevail (used with the permission of David Trevail)

LITTLE WATER

Little Water is a hamlet off the A30 on the Goonhavern to Perranporth Road. What follows was related by one of the residents, a Cornishman born and bred.

There are many jokes that play on the similarity of the words *goat* and *ghost*. This story isn't a joke. It is an account of an incident that happened to an eleven-year-old boy named David Trevail in 1950. Like many country children, David helped out on the farm at an early age. This particular day he had been driving a tractor – there were no rules and regulations then. On his way home, walking down the middle of a road that seldom saw any traffic, he saw a black and white, rough-furred billy goat in front of him. No one in the area kept goats! David continued and approached the goat, which was standing in the road opposite the ruins of an old cottage. When he was within a few yards of it the goat vanished into thin air. Whether this apparition was the ghost of a goat kept by the former owners of the old cottage, no one knows. The overgrown shell of the old cottage can still be seen by the side of the road today.

WADEBRIDGE

Wadebridge is a north Cornwall town that bestrides the River Camel, with a bridge that was built over the original wading crossing in the fifteenth century. The bridge has seventeen arches along its 320-foot length and is well worth a visit.

Wadebridge has numerous eerie stories. One that has been told many times and is certainly worth mentioning again is an

Molesworth Arms Hotel, Wadebridge

anniversary haunting. On the 31 December, at midnight, a phantom coach materialises in the courtyard of the Molesworth Arms Hotel, a sixteenth century coaching inn. The creepy coach leaves via the hallway; it is drawn by four horses and driven by a headless coachman. Several people claim to have seen it while others say they just heard it. It could be worth checking out on New Year's Eve at the midnight hour!

Phantom coaches are definitely popular in and around this old market town. On the night of a full moon another apparition of a coach and horses is reputed to race across Trewornan Bridge.

Does a ghostly rabbit visit the churchyard at Egloshayle Church?

Egloshayle Church, situated on a road beside the River Camel, faces across to the town of Wadebridge. Despite the church having a strong bellringing tradition, this does not seem to have frightened away the ghostly white rabbit that some claim to have seen gambolling around the churchyard before disappearing into the wall.

As traditions go, where there are rabbits there will be someone who wants to take a pot shot at them. A local man with a shotgun went out hunting the ghostly rabbit at Egloshayle Church. A few of his friends who were curious about how he would get on followed at a safe distance. They heard the gun go off and raced to the scene, only to find the hunter dead, shot by his own gun. The ghost of this tragic victim now also haunts the churchyard. It can be seen pointing a gun at something disturbing grasses in the distance.

ROCHE ROCK

This iconic granite outcrop, with its ruined chapel ingeniously incorporating the bedrock as its foundation, is a must-see. The chapel is two storeys high and was dedicated to St Michael in 1409. Climb up the iron ladders to the top of the chapel and experience the wind howling across the heathland. Cast your mind back to the 1982 film *Omen, The Final Conflict*; this site

The ruined chapel at Roche Rock

was one of the filming locations, the perfect spooky setting for a story of the unknown.

Jan Tregeagle, a wicked sixteenth century lawyer who was sent to hell for his sins but then reprieved and given impossible tasks to do, fled to Roche Rock hoping for sanctuary in the chapel, but the demon dogs of hell pursued him. Now the doomed spirit of Tregeagle wanders forever – listen out for him screaming above the storm.

Another manifestation of a man is alleged to appear staring down from the lofty chapel, and others have reported seeing what they understand to be the same figure flitting like a shadow among the rocks. Locals say he is a murdered miner or smuggler, while others maintain he is the ghost of a leper who used the lower room of the chapel like a hermitage, living there while being looked after by his daughter Gundred who brought him food and water from a holy well.

ST GERMANS

St Germans is located in southeast Cornwall on the River Tiddy, a part of the estuary of the Lynher which joins the Tamar near Saltash. Port Eliot Festival, held in the grounds of the Earl of St German's Cornish estate, is a great attraction; the festival offers a rich diversity of music and literature once a year in the summer.

Equally as well known as the Port Eliot Festival, but more infamous, is the tale of Dando of St Germans, reputed to be a dissolute fourteenth century priest – or, as he is described locally, *Dando was a 'eller for the women and he liked a drop of the hard stuff.* The story goes that one Sunday morning, instead of attending to his religious duties he encouraged his followers to go out on a hunt with him and his hounds. There were many stops for liquid refreshment of an alcoholic nature, and when the wine ran out Dando shouted for more. A stranger dressed all in black and riding a black hunter joined the group at that point, and it was he that offered a cup of wine. Dando downed the cup in one. He smacked his lips and said, 'That was the nectar of the gods.'

The man made a mock bow and replied in an informative tone, 'Or the devil!'

'If that was a drink of the devil,' the drunken priest remarked with a laugh, 'then may I go to hell!'

At these words the man in black leaned forward and grabbed hold of Dando; he flung the priest across his saddle and spurred his horse forward. The black hunter sped away carrying the screaming Dando and followed by the yelping pack of hounds. The man in black rode the horse into the river. The water hissed and sprayed and soon covered the horse, the rider and the by now demented priest.

There are many that listen on a Sunday for the ghost of Dando calling to his hounds, and for his screams over the sounds of a horse galloping to hell.

CAMBORNE

This town in the west of the Duchy was once of great importance for tin and copper mining. It is also well known

Camborne Church

for the engineer Richard Trevithick (1771–1833) who invented and demonstrated the Puffing Devil, a steam-powered locomotive celebrated in the song *Goin' up Camborne Hill*.

Parts of Camborne Church may date from the twelfth or thirteenth centuries, but it was in the 1940s that a visitation was witnessed which takes some explaining. Late one evening two figures in white appeared near the tower; they proceeded silently through the churchyard gate and continued down the adjacent Rectory Road.

Another reputed sighting in the same vicinity saw a procession of people dressed in black and wearing three-cornered hats. Others may have observed these sightings, but no one is on record for it.

CAMBORNE-REDRUTH BYPASS

In the 1980s a man was driving down this bypass at around two o'clock in the morning. Suddenly in the headlights of his car he saw a woman and a child crossing the road in front of him. He braked and immediately got out of the car, convinced he would find two casualties in the road. There was nothing. He glanced at the embankment at the side of the road and saw the misty figures of a woman and child disappearing over the top of the embankment.

REDRUTH

Like its sister town of Camborne, Redruth has many mining links. It is the home of Kresenn Kernow, the Cornish studies centre, and it takes great pride in the fact that a house in Cross Street was where the inventor William Murdock first installed gas lighting.

A curious dialect phrase used to be employed in the town. When anyone sees a ghost they say *Nummy dummy*. This is an obvious corruption of *In nomine Domini* (in the name of the Lord), a shortened form of the invocation used in blessing oneself with the sign of the cross.

TRURO

The cathedral city of Cornwall was one of the original stannary towns. Today Truro is a very busy shopping centre offering locals and visitors a wide range of shops in which to spend their

The Cathedral in Truro

money. Alternatively there are many pubs, clubs and hotels that offer a warm welcome. There is one place in particular that could offer readers of books like this a spirit or two... The William IV pub in Kenwyn Street is thought to have been built on the site of a friary. The previous occupants apparently visit on occasions. A former pub, the Star in Castle Street, was troubled by the spirit of a girl who was murdered nearby.

LAUNCESTON

This town is known as Lanson to those who are Cornish born and bred. Described as the gateway to Cornwall, its Norman castle dominates the town. Once there was a busy railway station in Launceston. Even though the tracks have been removed, several people have reported that the sound of steam can still be heard, and a phantom goods train has been witnessed passing through.

There are also reports of a ghoul haunting the St Mary Magdalene churchyard in Launceston.

CONSTANTINE

The village of Constantine, named after a sixth century priest, is situated between Falmouth and Helston. An article headlined *A Courageous Ghost* was reported in the Royal Cornwall Gazette on Friday 3 September 1880. A party of workmen from Helston were returning from a walk in Constantine one Wednesday evening when they were confronted by a spectre dressed in white with rattling chains. The party gave chase to the ghost through several fields and caught a tablecloth, which they bore off in triumph. The ghost, alarmed at the loss of its cloth, followed the group and begged for it back; the cloth was duly returned. Being an appendage of a ghost it was suggested that perhaps such a curiosity should have gone to a museum.